Our Mountains to Climb

A Journey of Love and Faith through Trials

Barbara J. Corcoran

ISBN 978-1-63575-972-3 (Paperback)
ISBN 978-1-63575-973-0 (Digital)

Christian Faith Publishing, Inc.
296 Chestnut Street
Meadville, PA 16335
www.christianfaithpublishing.com

Printed in the United States of America

I would like to dedicate this book to my husband, Bob, whose life motivated me to write his inspiring story. His continual encouragement and unwavering support greatly assisted me during the writing process.

May this book be a testament of my deep respect and unconditional love for him.

Acknowledgments

I would like to thank my close friend, Valerie, for helping me proof and edit my autobiography. Thank you for believing in my story and giving me the courage to move forward to publish my first book.

I would also like to thank all those whose suggestion that I write a book about our story sparked a desire in me to document how God has brought us through our trials.

Thank you to Bob's brother, Ron, and his mom, Dot, and my friends Clois and Patty who encouraged me through the writing process.

Contents

1: Looking Back 9

2: The Wedding Dress Promise 11

3: God Brings Us Together 13

4: The Diagnosis 18

5: The Engagement 22

6: Wedding Plans 25

7: Our Big Day 29

8: The Honeymoon 33

9: A Period of Preparation 35

10: The Transplant 38

11: A Time of Healing......................................45

12: Another Mountain 54

13: The Party 58

14: Our Climb Continues 60

15: Valley of Rest...64

16: Looking Forward.......................................66

Epilogue 71

1

Looking Back

FOR SEVERAL MONTHS, I was busy with all the arrangements for my husband Bob's surprise birthday party, all while trying to keep it a secret from him. As I sat at the airport waiting for his mother's plane to arrive from Florida, I thought of how fortunate Bob was to be here in 2015, about to celebrate his sixtieth birthday. I began to reflect back on what God had brought us through in the past sixteen years with his health issues. That brought to mind a life lesson that God taught me twenty years ago.

I had traveled to China for a mission trip with Grace Church. The next year, I felt God's call to go back to China that summer to teach oral English in a university there. While preparing for the trip, I was informed that instead of being assigned to a university, I would be teaching inspection officers at a police academy near Beijing, China.

As I was standing at my kitchen sink, I began questioning whether I was ready for this challenge. Then God reminded me of the summer before when my team and I had the awesome opportunity to tour the Great Wall of China. We were walking up a straight incline when a team member told me to turn around and look back to see how far we had climbed. I was amazed to see how high up we had hiked. We were so captivated by the amazing view that we didn't even notice the climb.

Ahead of us were many steep steps up to a watchtower. A friend noticed that I was getting tired and suggested that I might want to stay there and wait for them while they continued on up. I said that I had not come this far to not complete the journey to the top. The breathtaking view from the tower of the Great Wall winding its way across the high mountain peaks and into the distance was well worth the climb.

As I looked out my kitchen window, I was picturing that scene again in my mind, as God told me to look back at how far He had brought me and then look forward to what He had ahead for me. Sometimes God calls us to do a job that is outside of our comfort zone, but He is not going to ask us to do a task without equipping us for it. What a great blessing and incredible experience I would have missed if I had not answered His call.

This lesson also applies to whatever mountain of difficulties we are faced with in life. God has not brought us this far to leave us. We must keep climbing while still looking to Him for our strength and courage, remembering to always appreciate the view and adventure He has provided along life's journey.

After reflecting on this lesson, I remembered that it was around that time that our story began with a promise from God.

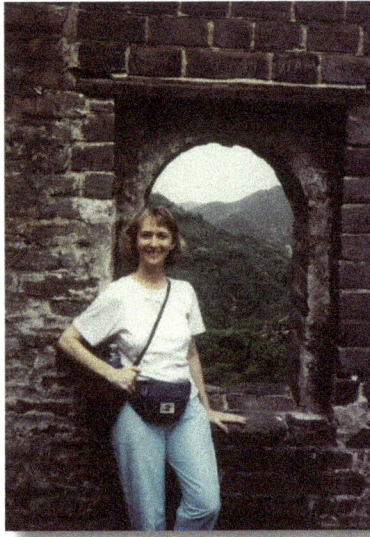

Barbara in the watch tower on the Great Wall of China

2

The Wedding Dress Promise

I ALWAYS THOUGHT that I would finish college, teach elementary school for a year or two, and then get married and raise a family.

To my surprise, I found myself a couple of decades later in my midforties, still a single teacher, and with no family of my own.

Amy, a dear friend of mine, called and began to inform me of the challenges that she and her family were facing. They were having some financial difficulties since she quit teaching to stay home with their young son. She told me that she would look for opportunities to bring in a little extra income to help out her family. She planned to sell her wedding dress, until she felt that God had told her to keep it for me to wear at my wedding in the future. I reminded her that I was not presently seeing anyone, and there were not even any prospects at that time.

Showing that she was not discouraged, she repeated what she strongly felt God had revealed to her. Then she asked if she could bring the dress over for me to try on that afternoon. Not wanting to disappoint her, I reminded Amy that she was 5'7" and thin, and I was 5'4" and not as thin. She quickly let me know that I could have it altered.

So she promptly arrived with the garment bag and opened it to reveal the elegant ivory satin dress with a lace-covered bodice sprinkled with sequins and pearls. A long beautiful train outlined with lace and a delicate lace inlay in the center flowed out from behind the dress as it cascaded onto the floor. It was everything I could have imagined for my wedding gown.

Then as I tried on the dress, it was obvious that it was too small for me because the row of small satin buttons in the back could not be fastened. As a seamstress myself, I knew that it is much easier to alter a garment that is too big than one that is far too small. My concern did not affect Amy because she stood firm in what she believed. She knew that if God had a plan for that dress, He would work it out.

As I stood looking in the mirror at myself in the lovely wedding gown, it was confirmed to Amy that she was to save it for me. So she carefully packed the dress back into its protective bag and confidently took it home to be stored for the special day that He had predicted.

I put the thought of Amy's wedding dress on the shelf until God would reveal His promise to me.

3

God Brings Us Together

A FEW YEARS later, I was invited to attend a young singles' Sunday school class at Grace Church. I informed them that I was well above the age limit for that class, but I was assured that age did not matter and that I would enjoy it there.

In the past, I had a hard time finding a singles' class in my age group where I felt comfortable because almost everyone else was a single divorced parent. The class was a place of refuge for them because they were with others who understood what they were going through. I, on the other hand, was the one who was different.

But in the younger class, most of them, like me, had never been married. They also encouraged me to come to their fellowships and convinced me that I belonged in their group. Even though I thought I would not meet anyone old enough to be a prospective future husband, I enjoyed Sunday school and all of their fun activities and fellowships.

One Sunday after class, I looked around and noticed a new face. I immediately thought, *Oh, there is someone else who does not belong in this class*. To my surprise, he proceeded to come across the room to introduce himself to me. Then I overheard him complimenting the Sunday school teacher on his lesson, and I thought to myself, *He must be an encourager*.

After I talked to a group of friends in the hallway, I started down the hall to the worship service. As the newcomer, Bob, came out of the classroom to greet those still standing there, I glanced over my shoulder and again thought to myself, *There is something different about this guy.*

I saw Bob again that week at a Bible study at a class member's home. As I walked into the kitchen, Bob said hello to me as he cut into his piece of the ice cream pie that I had brought. The plate and pie flipped out of his hand and onto his shirt and landed on the floor. I apologized that my graham cracker crust was too hard to cut easily as I quickly served him another piece.

Then we sat down at the table, and he began to tell me that he grew up in New York and Vermont. In the early 1980s, he moved here to the Tulsa area to attend Rhema Bible Training Center. Due to their teaching, after he graduated, he founded a nonprofit organization and became the executive director of Helping Hands of Tulsa, an agency that worked with local low-income youth.

Since Bob organized and instructed tennis clinics with the children in the recreational centers, he was asked to plan one as an activity for our Sunday school class at a nearby park. We had a large turnout. He began by teaching tennis skills through the use of fun games. Next, we took turns hitting tennis balls over the net. Then we were ready to get into teams to play doubles.

At this time, one of the men from the class called a friend of his who played tennis to come join us. When the friend and his wife arrived, he suggested that his friend play against Bob. After a while, the visitor turned around and announced to his friend, "Hey, this guy is good!"

His friend laughed and informed him, "He should be. He was a professional tennis instructor and played on the pro tennis tour for a year."

"Oh, you got me," he laughingly replied.

A couple of weeks later, the Sunday school class's activities director called to inform me about the class-sponsored bowling trip for the youth from Bob's agency. She asked if I would like to pay for a child's bowling fee and mentor a group of children as they bowled.

Since it was the Saturday after my school would be dismissed for the summer, I gladly agreed.

At the bowling alley, a group of rowdy boys were assigned to my lane. To my relief, Bob's younger brother, Ron, who worked for the agency, sat at the counter behind us to help monitor the boys.

Ron told me that he had moved here to Oklahoma to work with his brother. While working with children from the agency, Ron decided to go back to college to get a second degree in elementary education. He had just graduated and would start teaching that fall in a school where some of the agency's youth attended.

The bowling event was a great success. Afterward, Bob transported the children back to the center, and then he joined our group at a restaurant for dinner. He sat across from me and asked me what my plans were for the summer. I told him that I was looking for a local ministry where I could volunteer my time. Since I had spent my last three summers on mission trips to China, I knew it was important to keep busy doing some form of volunteer work here at home. Bob told me that his agency might need my help.

A week or two later, the Sunday school class's activities director gave me a list of people to call to inform them of an upcoming class event. Bob happened to be on that list, and when I called him, he asked if I could fill in for a volunteer who would not be able to continue with the kid's summer tennis program. I accepted the offer, and in addition to tennis, my summer was filled with sponsoring field trips and a variety of events with the children.

Even after school started back, I continued to help with weekend field trips and activities. In return, Bob did a tennis clinic field trip for my third grade class during their PE class time. Our PE teacher, Martha, came to the park with us to assist Bob with his program. My students thoroughly enjoyed this fun sport.

Through all of the volunteering, Bob and I developed a strong friendship, even though we were not dating.

Several months later, my parents came for a weekend visit. Bob joined us at a restaurant where he was able to get acquainted with my mom and dad.

A week later, I received an upsetting call informing me that Dad had been in an accident on his bicycle. He had collided with a car as he was turning into his driveway. Then while in the emergency waiting room, my mom had a cardiac arrest and was resuscitated.

By the time I arrived at the hospital, I found both Dad and Mom in ICU in rooms next to each other. Dad was in traction because of a crushed pelvis. He also hit his head on the pavement during the accident, which may have caused him to be disoriented. So he did not understand the reason for the traction, and he would look at it to figure out how to untie the ropes. He was so proud when he released himself from traction, as though he were an escape artist. The physical therapist would have to come in to hook it up again, so they asked our family to stay with him at all times to try to distract him from the confining equipment.

When Mom was resuscitated, it broke her rib, which collapsed her lung. So a breathing tube was placed down her throat. Mom also had to be watched because she would try to pull out the breathing tube since it was very uncomfortable.

The doctor did not think Mom would make it. He and the nurses said that she should not have been resuscitated because it was too much from which to recover for someone of her age. My sister said, "But he does not know our mother. She is a trooper!" We were not surprised when the doctor gave us the report that Mom did pull through and soon after was dismissed from the hospital.

Several years later, Mom would say, "I know I survived so I could take care of your dad."

After Dad's extensive stay in the hospital, I was given the news that he would be released soon. The doctor suggested that Dad should go into a nursing home. I asked the doctor if he would sign for Dad to be admitted to a physical therapy rehab. He agreed to sign, but said that it was not necessary because he felt that Dad would never walk again. I could not accept this diagnosis because Dad was always so active, and I knew he would give it all that he had.

There was not a physical therapy rehab facility close to them, and my mom did not drive, so I found a rehab near to where I lived in Tulsa that would admit him.

A former third grade student of mine was going to a local university to receive a degree in physical therapy. She happened to be observing the physical therapist at the hospital on the day that Dad was released. Since Dad was still nonweight bearing, the physical therapist had to lift him out of the wheelchair and into my car.

It was comforting to have her there with me. It was hard to watch Dad hollering out in confusion because he didn't understand what was happening. As she assured me with her words and presence, I knew that she would make a great physical therapist.

Then I drove Dad straight to the rehab facility, which was a two-hour drive. Several therapists met us at the car and smoothly transferred him to a wheelchair and took him to his room.

Then Mom came home with me to stay while Dad was at the rehab. After Dad was released from the facility, a physical therapist came to my house to continue working with him. When Dad completed all of his treatments, he did defy the odds and was able to walk again with the help of a walker. Unfortunately, Dad continued to be disoriented and was later diagnosed with Alzheimer's disease.

Mom decided it would be best for them to continue to live with me because she did not want to leave the great care they were receiving from their new doctors. I found myself very busy with teaching, caring for my parents, and volunteering for Bob's agency.

Bob and I were unaware that our friendship would deepen due to unforeseen events in the months to come.

4

The Diagnosis

LATER THAT YEAR, Bob began noticing alarming symptoms. He could hardly catch his breath after climbing one flight of stairs in his condo. When he nicked himself while shaving, it was difficult to stop the bleeding. Bob was waiting to go to the doctor until his agency would be able to afford health insurance for their full-time employees in a few months.

But before that happened, he woke up with spots before his eyes, which impaired his vision. This concerned Bob enough that he went to his eye doctor that day. The doctor said that his eyes were fine, but he suggested that he go to a primary care doctor to get a blood test taken.

After his lab work came back, he received a call from the doctor telling him to go to the emergency room immediately to get a blood transfusion. When Bob arrived at the ER, the doctor there firmly suggested that he should be admitted to the hospital first before the transfusion so they could run tests to discover what was causing all of his blood counts to be so extremely low.

Several days later, I was the one Bob asked to join him at his hospital room when the doctor was going to give him the test results. So I told my school that I would be a little late for work that morning. I was glad I was there with Bob as the doctor informed him of his stage 4 lymphoma cancer that was in his spleen and had spread to his bone morrow. The doctor asked Bob, "What did you do last weekend?"

Bob proudly answered, "Oh, I played in the finals of a tennis tournament with my brother."

"That's what I thought," answered the doctor. "How often do you exercise?"

Bob answered, "Oh, every day. When I feel tired, I exercise, and it gives me the energy to keep going."

The doctor began to explain. "The average person with blood counts as low as yours would have been in bed for months and unable to do much. It has been your athletic mind-set that has kept you going."

Then Bob was informed that the next step would be surgery to remove his spleen, and then he would begin six months of chemotherapy.

I left the hospital in a daze as I drove to school. When I walked to my classroom, I felt too overwhelmed to enter and begin teaching. My class was doing well, so I went to the second grade classroom where the class was busy working, and the teacher, Donna, was talking to a student. I knocked and asked if I could speak to her.

She came to the door and stood in the doorway so she could keep an eye on her class as she listened to me share my sad news. I could not hold back the tears as I said that I couldn't bear the thought of losing my good friend. Donna gave me a hug and then began praying for Bob and me.

I wiped away my tears, and then I was ready to go to my classroom. I was so thankful that I was teaching in a Christian school and for the teacher who took the time to help me through a difficult day.

Bob's one-week stay in the hospital for tests and transfusion racked up a total of $11,000 in bills. As soon as one of his board members heard of Bob's situation, he immediately applied for insurance for the full-time employees of the agency. Even though Bob's cancer was preexisting, he would be covered because he was, as they called it, getting in on the ground floor.

It would take three weeks before the start-up date, so Bob told his doctor he needed to hold off on his surgery until he was covered by insurance. The doctor told Bob that he could wait three weeks only because his red and white blood cells and platelets were so dangerously low. He could bleed to death from a nosebleed or a small cut. Bob was advised to restrict his activity until the surgery.

Even though Bob was now covered by insurance, he still had the $11,000 total in bills that he owed for his first hospital visit. They let Bob pay a certain amount each month. Then he received a call about one of the individual bills. They said if he paid it before the beginning of the year, they would charge him less. So he called about some of the other individual bills to see what the payoff would be for them.

My school had a special offering for Bob. The teachers kept a jar on their desks for anyone who wanted to give change. The total amount given was $250. One of Bob's bills was close to $500, but they told him that they would accept $250 if he paid it off immediately. I was able to explain to the students how God provided through their giving the exact amount that Bob needed. Before long, he was able to get it all paid off.

Bob's parents, Jim and Dot, had planned to go on a cruise at about the time that Bob was diagnosed. They talked to the doctor on the phone to see if they needed to cancel their plans. He told them that it was serious and recommended that they come right away. So they immediately drove from Florida to Tulsa to be with Bob until after his surgery. Soon after they arrived, they went with Bob to his surgeon's appointment. The surgeon explained in full detail all that was involved in removing his spleen.

Later that evening, Bob took a walk with his mom. He expressed his concern and hesitancy in having the surgery. Dot reminded him that if he did not have his spleen removed, he would not live long, so it was worth the risk. Dot's talk reassured him and gave him the courage to move forward with the necessary surgery.

Through all of this, Bob and I began to realize how deeply we felt about each other. The night before Bob was to go back into the hospital, he told me, "If I make it through the surgery, I want to talk about the possibility of a future for us."

When I drove home that night, I was filled with a range of emotions. I wanted to shout for joy at the prospect of marriage, and then I was about to cry at the thought of losing my best friend. As I held the steering wheel in my hand and stared at the road before me and not knowing what might lie ahead in the future for us, I realized I wanted to spend whatever time Bob had left with him.

Later, I read in a marriage book that love is a decision. When you meet the right person for you who has the character matched with your character that no matter what happens in life, you can make the decision each day to love them through the good and difficult times. This suddenly all made sense to me. I had always heard that you don't have a choice of whom you love because it is something that happens to you. But actually, the decision is ours; even though it may not be an easy one at times, it is the correct one if we are the right one for each other.

I then understood the strong mixed feelings that I had that night as I traveled home. They came from a love that grew out of a strong mutual friendship and developed into an unconditional love that can weather the strongest storm.

5

The Engagement

B OB'S SURGERY WAS a success. The doctor said that his spleen was the size of a football instead of the normal size of a fist, and that he was fortunate it had not ruptured.

After a week of recovery, Bob kept his promise, and we began talking about our future. We decided to take our time because of all that he was going through.

After Thanksgiving, his parents went back to Florida. Shortly after Christmas, Bob began six months of chemo. On Sunday, Valentine's Day, Bob took me out to a nice Italian restaurant for dinner where, to my surprise, he pulled out a beautiful engagement ring and asked me to marry him. He then took me to another nearby restaurant for dessert. Next on his agenda, he took me across the street to the mall to go shopping. He wanted to make it a special day for me.

First we told our families. I was surprised that his family already knew what Bob planned to give me for Valentine's. Bob bought my ring from his brother-in-law, Chuck, who owned a jewelry store in New York.

I could not wait until school the next day to announce the news. Before school, I showed a couple of teachers my special gift. More teachers from down the hall and around the corner came when they heard the excitement and huddled around me to see the ring.

When class started, I asked my students to guess what I received for Valentine's Day. They began to guess the usual flowers, candy, and card as I waved my left hand in the air. Finally, a student hollered out, "Oh, you got a ring!"

"Yes," I replied. "Mr. Bob gave me an engagement ring!" They knew him as Mr. Bob because he did a tennis clinic for my class.

The class squealed with delight as I walked around the room to give them an up-close look at my special gift. Then a student asked, "Does that mean that when you get married, your name will be Mrs. Bob?"

I held back a grin as I told them his last name.

A few days later, Bob stopped by the school to visit me. Debbie, a former music teacher at our school, met us on the stairway with a cake for us that had the words "We Are Going to the Chapel" written across it in frosting. It was such a sweet surprise. Then the teachers had a chance to congratulate Bob.

We decided to get married after Bob finished chemo treatments in June. First, we needed to schedule counseling at Grace. After we completed the four weeks of counseling, we could then set the wedding date for the ceremony at our church.

Once we began counseling, it was time for me to find a place for my mom and dad near Bob's condo because I would be moving there after we were married. Mom said she wanted to rent a duplex. I showed her all of the duplexes within three miles of Bob's condo, and then we had to wait for one to come open.

Just a few days later, I saw a For Lease sign in front of a duplex that was just a block or two from Bob's place. I couldn't believe my eyes because it was the perfect location for them. Later, Mom said many times that out of all the units on that street, it was her favorite one because of its layout. She also liked that it was next to the highway and she could watch the cars go by, and since her unit was on the other side of the duplex, her backyard was not next to the highway. She was very thankful for how everything worked out.

On weekends, my parents and I drove two hours to their house where they had lived for thirty-seven years to pack up their belongings that they wanted to keep and prepare the rest for an auction. In

March when the packing was completed, we had movers load their furniture and belongings into the moving van and drive it to the duplex, where Mom and Dad were able to get moved during my spring break.

After my parents' auction, I also had to get their house ready to put up for sale. Dad, who was a carpenter and contractor, had built it himself, so this was a task filled with mixed emotions for all of us. I found a realtor and got their house on the market. After one offer fell through, they received another offer that they accepted. I was relieved that we would not have to go down there for the closing, but could take care of it here by fax.

I also had to get my house fixed up and ready to sell.

Once our marriage counseling was completed, we were able to set the wedding date for June 19, which gave me only three months to make all of the arrangements.

6

Wedding Plans

THERE WAS ONE wedding detail I didn't have to worry about. The day I got engaged, I called my friend Amy, who now lived a three-hour drive away. The next day she happily drove up with her wedding dress and even her matching wedding shoes.

A friend at work told me about a lady who sewed wedding dresses in her home, which was outside of the city. It was a drive over there for all of the fittings, but to my relief, she was able to do the necessary alterations for the dress to fit me.

During my spring break, I went shopping to find a dress for my mom for the wedding. I found the perfect light-peach two-piece dress. I bought it, and I couldn't wait to take it to Mom to have her try it on to see if she liked it. She was delighted with my choice. It was just the right fit, and it was so pretty on her.

While I was shopping, I stopped at a bridal shop even though I already had a dress. I just wanted to have fun trying on dresses. The clerk had me stand on a riser and look at myself in the mirror. A teenager who was looking for a prom dress walked by, looked up at me, and stopped. She asked me with a surprise in her voice, "You're getting married?!"

Deciding to not be offended, I answered back, "Yes, I am getting married! It is never too late."

"Oh, that's nice," she replied in an understanding voice.

I did not find a dress that I liked as well as Amy's dress, but I was glad that I took the time to finally enjoy the experience of wedding gown shopping.

The next step was to find a floral shop to arrange the flowers for the ceremony, but everyone I called was already booked for June. I knew that meant I would have to shop for and arrange silk flowers. The thought of doing all of that was overwhelming for me.

Then a teacher I worked with, whose wedding was the summer before, told me her mom was still storing the flowers she used for centerpieces on the tables at her wedding reception. She said I could have them and her ivory pew bows for my wedding. I could hardly believe it when she told me. They were ivory roses, and I wanted ivory and pink roses. With pink floral spray paint, I would be able to have the flowers I was hoping to have for my wedding. I just didn't know how I would get them arranged into bouquets and corsages.

A new lady in my Sunday school class walked up to me and began to tell me that she had arranged flowers for a couple of her friends' weddings. She offered her services if I needed it.

What a blessing she was! She did a great job with the flowers. For my bouquet, she made an ivory satin fan that represented my trips to China. To the fan she attached a beautiful arrangement that she made with the pink and ivory roses. She also took charge of decorating the church and reception hall and even ran some last-minute errands for me.

The photographers were also booked for June. One of the photographers I called told me about someone he knew who might be willing to work a wedding again, since he had taken some time off. I contacted him, and he agreed to take the job. I was very thankful to have beautiful photos of our special day.

Then six weeks before the wedding, my dad had an emergency colostomy surgery due to a twisted colon. Part of his colon was removed and a colostomy bag was attached. He was in the hospital for a month. Mom stayed with me during that time. She would take a taxi to the hospital each day, and after school, I would go to see Dad and bring Mom home with me. The doctor could not tell me when or if Dad would recover from the surgery. He said it was a difficult surgery for even a young person to go through.

Finally, to our relief, Dad suddenly pulled through. Two nurses gave Mom and me a training session on how to care for his colostomy bag because he didn't understand what it was all about. Then Dad was dismissed from the hospital two weeks before my wedding. So Mom and I happily went shopping to buy a suit for him to wear to the ceremony, and then we picked him up from the hospital and took him home to their duplex.

The cakes at the bakery that was recommended to me cost more than I felt I should spend. However, I was fortunate to find just what I wanted from a local grocery store bakery. Altogether, a beautiful wedding cake and two square groom's cakes cost the same as what the wedding cake alone would have cost at the other bakery.

A close friend, Valerie, whose husband is a farmer, offered to furnish the peanuts that they grew on their farm. She also made mint candy and poured it into rose-shaped molds.

The last item I wanted for the reception table was chocolate-covered strawberries. My sister planned to dip the strawberries for me. Then a week before the wedding, she said she would not be able to arrive in time to do it.

That week I received a call from a lady who had attended my Sunday school class before she got married. She had just heard about our wedding. She wanted to know if there was something she could do to help with it. I let her know that I needed someone who could dip the strawberries. She said she would love to do that for me, and she would furnish the strawberries and chocolate as our wedding gift. She even brought them on a silver-colored platter to the reception room for me.

Every detail fell into place at just the right time. I knew it was not just a coincidence. This reminded me of a clock that I saw years before that had the words "God's Timing Is Perfect" written across the clock's face. This confirmed to us that we did not need to worry about tomorrow because He held our future in His hands.

Due to Bob's first hospital bill, we had a very limited budget for the wedding. But because of people coming forward to help us out for every detail of the ceremony and reception, we were able to put together a beautiful event for a surprisingly minimal amount of money. The Lord truly blessed us.

7

Our Big Day

BOB HAD JUST completed his six months of chemo, and his doctor's appointment was on the day of our wedding rehearsal! Bob's parents and Aunt Ann arrived from Florida and came with us to the doctor's office. He informed us that after the honeymoon, Bob would need to begin six more months of chemo, but it would not cure his type of lymphoma. He also stated that he had "something else up his sleeve" that he would discuss at his next appointment.

With the doctor's visit still in the back of our minds, we went to our rehearsal. The rehearsal and dinner went well. Visiting with family and friends who came from out of town to be a part of this special event helped us keep our focus on our big day ahead.

It rained the morning of our wedding, but it did not dampen our spirits. That afternoon and just before guests arrived, the sun came out to greet everyone. I was delighted to hear that we had a large attendance of family, friends, coworkers, and several of my dear students who came to celebrate our special day with us.

My music teacher friend, Debbie, played the piano, and another music teacher friend, Laurie, sang for the ceremony. While our parents were seated, my friend Amy sang a lovely song that her dad had written. One of my former students played the trumpet while the groom and groomsmen entered the sanctuary. My great nephew, Tyler, did a great job as my ring bearer. My cute flower girl Hannah, the daughter of my friend Karen, dropped a path of rose petals as she entered and lit up the room with her smile.

As I walked into the chapel, I was so excited to see some of my sweet students sitting by the aisle that I almost tripped on my dress. I caught my balance as I looked ahead and saw Bob waiting for me. Amy, my matron of honor, helped adjust the train of the special wedding dress as I walked up the steps to the altar.

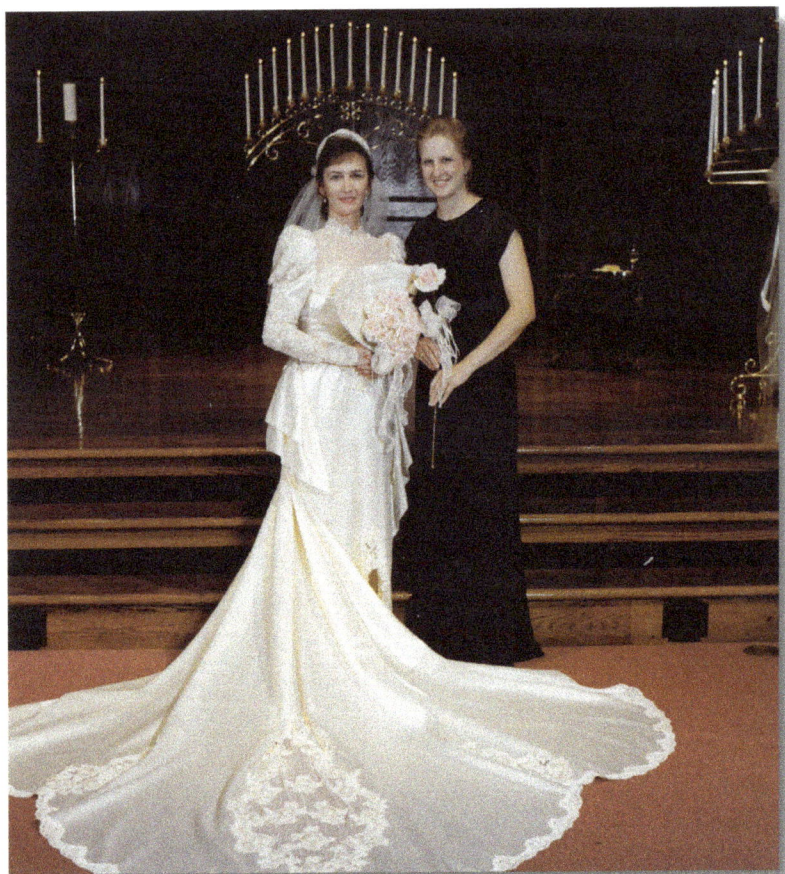

Barbara in "the wedding dress" with her matron of honor, Amy

The bride and groom on their big day

The ceremony and reception were beautiful and all that I hoped it would be. I wanted my wedding to be simple and elegant. It was that and even more. The music was beautiful, and the lovely songs that Laurie and Amy sang helped to tell our story. Everyone said that it was a touching and moving ceremony.

The reception table was beautifully adored with rose petals, and the lovely wedding cake that was decorated with pink roses and doves nestled on top. Valerie's homegrown roasted peanuts and homemade rose-shaped mint candies were a nice addition to the table.

On the groom's table were two square groom's cakes. One was decorated as a chess set because Bob was in a chess club in high school and enjoyed the game. At each corner of the other cake sat a big strawberry dressed up in a frosting tuxedo. The chocolate-dipped strawberries arranged on a silver-colored tray were placed next to the cake. Burgundy napkins with our names on them and a silver coffee and tea set helped to decorate the table.

31

Bob's brother Ron gave a beautiful toast. Then Bob and I cut the cake and politely fed each other. The guests lined up to greet us and then received their piece of cake. It was a festive time, and we enjoyed visiting with all who came to celebrate with us.

After the reception, Bob's dad chauffeured us in his Cadillac to Bob's condo, where our families were waiting for us with a special dinner that his family had prepared for the occasion. Then we opened our wedding presents, and Amy showed us a video that she had taken before the wedding ceremony and during the wedding reception. After a great visit, we said good-bye and left for our honeymoon.

8

The Honeymoon

FOR THE FIRST two nights, we stayed at a lovely bed-and-breakfast north of the city. We were so exhausted from everything going on in the last few months that this gave us time to rest up.

Then on Monday, we flew to Florida for a week. After our wedding, Bob's parents drove to New York to visit Bob's sister, Barbara, and her family for a month. While they were in New York, they had us stay at their house in Florida. On their kitchen counter we found gift cards to restaurants and a gas card so we could drive their other car while we were there. We were able to use the pool and whirlpool at their neighborhood clubhouse. Their addition also had a lake, where we took a guided tour on a pontoon to have lunch at a café on the lake. Their house was close to the beach and a two-hour drive from Orlando, so there were plenty of exciting places for us to go and things to do to make it a memorable trip.

On Thursday, we received a call from our real estate agent informing us that we had an offer on my house. She told us that at first, people were not interested because of cracks on the side and back of the house.

So on her own, she hired someone to fix the foundation, and then she increased the list price for the same amount that it cost for the repairs. She immediately received an offer for full price with a closing date at the end of July.

We were so excited. That gave me time to get my furniture and other possessions that I did not need ready for a garage sale and close on the house before school started. We were so thankful for our realtor and friend, who so efficiently worked everything out for us while we were away.

This was just another confirmation that God was there for us and would continue to guide us as we returned home to begin the next step in our journey.

9

A Period of Preparation

W E ARRIVED HOME the weekend of the Fourth of July. We had Bob's brother and my parents over for a barbeque at our condo. It was nice to get back from Florida and for me to get settled into my new home and life with my new husband.

When the holiday weekend was over, it was time to get back to reality as we arrived at Bob's much-anticipated appointment with his oncologist. He asked us how our wedding and honeymoon were, and then he proceeded to get down to business. The date was set to begin Bob's next six months of chemo.

Then the doctor began to reveal what he had "up his sleeve." He said the chemo would not cure Bob's type of lymphoma, but he felt that Bob would be a good candidate for a bone marrow transplant after he had completed the chemo. The transplant would be his only hope for remission, but he needed a sibling donor who was a match.

Bob began the next regiment of chemo treatments while we waited for Bob's two sisters and brother to be tested to receive the much-anticipated results. Finally to our relief, we discovered that both his sister, Kathleen, in Florida and his brother, Ron, who lived near us, were a match. The doctor said he felt Bob's brother would be the best donor because he was also a male, eleven years younger than Bob, and lived close by.

At first we thought we would have to go to Dallas for the transplant, which would mean I would have to take a leave of absence from school. Then Bob's doctor told us that an oncologist, Dr. Joseph Lynch, who had a bone morrow transplant unit back east, had recently moved here to set up one at our hospital.

At Bob's appointment with his new doctor, the transplant was scheduled for the middle of February. That would be a year since our Valentine engagement and eight months into our marriage. In the mean time, we tried to live in the present and make the most of our time.

Bob continued refereeing high school basketball. He would go in for a chemo treatment in the afternoon, and the nurse would bring in the bright blue IV bag that she referred to as "Smurf juice." Then with a wrap around the IV port in his wrist, that evening, he would go to referee a game.

As I sat in the bleachers, I could overhear parents complaining about the referees. I heard them say as they pointed to the other referee, "That referee doesn't know what he is doing." Then they pointed to Bob and stated, "And that one is just crazy!"

I thought to myself, *If only they knew all that Bob had gone through, they might have the respect and admiration for him that I have.*

My school's PE teacher, Martha, refereed some high school basketball games with Bob. She got tickets for us to a ladies' basketball game at TU, where she was working the shot clock. Bob was chosen to participate in a halftime activity, and he eagerly agreed. He had to make a three-point shot, a layup, and a free throw in just thirty seconds. Bob made the first two shots on his first try, but missed the free throw. He ran for the ball and quickly returned to the free throw line to try again. The audience counted down the last three seconds as the ball swished in the basket on the count of one. The crowd erupted in applause, unaware that he was going through chemo. Bob won a fifty-dollar gift card to a fancy restaurant, which was a great treat for us.

On weekends we would go to the lake to rest and recoup from everything going on during the week. We spent Thanksgiving in Branson, Missouri, where we stayed in a very nice log cabin, enjoyed

Thanksgiving dinner at Silver Dollar City, went to music shows, and just spent a wonderful time together.

Over Christmas vacation, we drove to Dallas to see a hockey game. A friend of ours got free tickets for us from the company where she worked. While in Dallas, we rode in a horse-drawn carriage, went to an aquarium, and made many new fond memories as we waited for the difficult road ahead of us.

10

The Transplant

READY OR NOT, in February, Bob was admitted to the bone marrow unit at Saint Francis Hospital to begin five days of high-dose chemotherapy and one round of full body radiation to kill out all of his bone marrow. Then he would start over with 10 percent of his brother's marrow.

After the first day of treatments, we left the hospital to go out to dinner with Ron to celebrate the first anniversary of our Valentine engagement. We thought it was all right to go, but the doctor said that even one day of the high-dose chemo lowered his resistance enough that he could have caught something that could have been serious for Bob. We felt bad, but we did have a good time. We knew that it would be quite a while before we would be able to go out to dinner again.

After they harvested Ron's bone marrow around his hips and into his bones, they brought it in an IV bag and set it up on the IV pole. They inserted it into the port in Bob's wrist the same as they would for a blood transfusion. The transplant itself is much easier on the recipient than the donor.

After the bone marrow was harvested, they were able to assign Ron to a room next door to Bob's in the bone marrow unit for recovery. That made it convenient for me. I would go back and forth to check on both of them and give a report to Bob and Ron on how the other one was doing.

That evening, Wednesday, when Ron was released from the hospital, I drove him home. He asked me to stop at the grocery store. Ron rode the store's electric wheelchair to shop for a few things that he would need while being laid up for the next several days. On Monday, although still very sore, Ron went back to work. He had to be on guard when his kindergarteners would try to give him a big hug.

Bob and Ron had different blood types, even though they were a bone marrow match. The doctor reported to us that he knew the transplant worked when Bob's blood type changed to that of Ron's. Bob has never forgotten nor failed to appreciate that he was able to beat cancer because of his brother.

The high-dose chemo and radiation brings the white blood cell count down to zero, and it takes time for it to build back to normal. The transplant patients are in a special unit, which is closed off from the other oncology rooms on that floor. Every time we entered the unit, we had to wash our hands thoroughly. If we were not feeling well, we could not visit and risk the chance that we may be catching something that might be contagious.

During this time, a young lady in the unit died from a cold or virus because of insufficient white cells to fight it off. This showed us just how serious the situation was.

On the last half day of school, the teachers went out for lunch. When we got back, as I walked by the office, I was informed that I had a message that Bob had come down with chicken pox. So I hurried to the hospital to check on Bob, who was very uncomfortable.

He had had the chicken pox when he was young, so the virus was still in his system. Normally the body builds up immunity, which keeps someone from coming down with the disease again. The transplant patient, however, does not have that immunity to fight off the virus. Anyone who had not previously had the chicken pox could not enter Bob's room because they would be susceptible to the virus. Fortunately, I had had the chicken pox as a child, so I was allowed to visit him. Several days later, Bob was able to recover from this setback.

At about the same time, Bob came down with a serious infection. When I talked to the specialist, he prepared me for the worse, but again Bob came through it.

Then Bob received the sad news that a close friend and board member of his agency had passed away from canccr. While Bob was having his radiation before the transplant, he saw his friend in the waiting room. He informed Bob that he was taking radiation too because he also had been diagnosed with cancer.

Hearing about his friend in addition to all that he had been going through caused Bob to start getting a little discouraged. I thought about a picture in a magazine of a resort in Corpus Christi that Bob had admired before he was hospitalized. The picture showed the lodge with several pools and the beach and ocean in the background. So I brought the picture to Bob to remind him of his wish to go to this beautiful resort. The nurse saw what I was doing and chimed in with encouragement. This took his mind off the present and gave him an incentive to get through all the difficult days ahead.

Then what we had feared would happen did come to pass. Bob's colon started rejecting his brother's bone marrow, which caused him to bleed severely through his colon. Even though he was on antirejection medication, the rejection lasted for a couple of months.

A friend told me that she was going through a difficult time, but she thought it was small compared to what Bob and I were going through. I told her that it was her mountain, and you cannot compare mountains. When you are at the foot of your own mountain looking up at what you have to climb, it looks overwhelming. You may look at someone else's mountain and say that you could not deal with what they are going through. Thankfully, God gives us the grace we need when we need it and not before.

I could not have gone through all of this without Bob's mom, who was my angel. Two weeks after the transplant, she came from Florida and stayed with me to help with Bob for three months until school was out for the summer. In the morning, she drove to the hospital for the day to help with Bob. I took a pair of jeans with me to school each day to change into after work so I could drive straight to the hospital and stay all evening. I usually arrived home between

9:30 p.m. to 10:00 p.m. Then Dot would come downstairs, and we would share with each other all that had happened while we were at the hospital. There was so much going on with Bob that it was easy for things to fall through the cracks.

One evening Bob wanted me to go to the cafeteria to buy him some grapefruit juice. At that time it was about the only thing that tasted good to him. Dot had just told me that she had overheard a visiting doctor say that grapefruit juice could interfere with the antirejection medication. I was thankful to have that information, but Bob was disappointed that he couldn't have grapefruit juice anymore.

One day I was running a little late getting to the hospital after work. Dot left knowing that I would be there soon because it was getting close to rush hour. When I arrived, I noticed everyone was rushing into Bob's room. They stopped me at the front desk and told me that Bob had fallen when he got up to go to the restroom. He had a deep cut above his eye, so a doctor had to come into his room to stitch it up. Bob's program director arrived and needed to talk to Bob about work, but he realized it would have to wait until later. Then when the doctor was finished and things settled down, I was finally able to go in to see Bob. There was never a dull moment around there.

To complicate things further, Bob had an allergic reaction to several of the strong medications that he was taking. One of his prescriptions gave him severe heart palpitations. I thought he was having a heart attack, but when his medicine was changed, the symptoms stopped.

When school let out for the summer, Dot went back to Florida. About two weeks later, Bob was released from inpatient to outpatient every day. I was told that they would not release him until he was off his IV, but Bob's insurance insisted that he be released as an inpatient due to the mounting cost.

That meant I would take him to the hospital at about seven thirty each morning. When we got there, they would do a blood check to see which electrolytes were low. Then he would receive them by IV. When the IV was completed, he could go home for the night.

It might be anywhere from 4:00 p.m. to sometimes as late as 7:30 p.m. before we could leave. The next morning, we would head for the hospital and do it all over again.

Bob had a twenty-four-hour IV for his antirejection medication, and at night I would have to give him a nutrition IV because he was not able to eat much. A home health nurse came out a few times to train me, and then I was on my own.

One night Bob woke me up to show me that his IV port had come out. I called the desk at his bone marrow unit at the hospital. The nurse said that since we would be coming to the hospital in a few hours, they could take care of it then. I was glad that I didn't have to drive him there at three in the morning.

Bob also had to give himself a shot in his stomach each day. When he got too weak to push in the needle, he asked me to do it for him. I had the nurses show me how so I could take over for Bob. I had always said that I had not missed my calling as a nurse. I never thought I could do all this myself, but sometimes you just do what you have to do, and the Lord gives the strength when you need it.

The full body radiation caused a deep layer of his skin to peel all over his body. Even though I was very tired, I would rub body lotion on his back, arms, and legs. One day Bob looked up at me and said, "Thank you for marrying me." His deep appreciation gave me the strength to continue caring for him.

By the end of the summer, the social worker on the oncology floor could see that I was wearing down. She told me I needed to take off for a couple of days to rest up before school started that fall. When I spoke to Bob about it, he agreed and suggested that I go to Grand Lake. He knew that being at the lake was relaxing for me. Then his brother stopped by the hospital for a visit and offered to stay with Bob while I was gone.

It was hard to leave, but I knew it would be best for everyone concerned. I realized how much I needed the rest when I woke up thinking I heard Bob calling to me. But after two days of resting, reading, and praying, I was ready to return home to see Bob and get my classroom ready for school to start. When I went back to teaching, Bob's mom arrived again, ready to help.

Finally, to our great relief, Bob's body finally accepted Ron's bone marrow, and he was released from his outpatient visits to the hospital. As we looked back at the last six months, we knew that it was only through prayer, the great care given by the doctors and nurses, the help of family and friends, and Bob's positive attitude and faith in God that got us through it all. When Bob was in the hospital, Dr. Lynch would come into the room and ask how he was feeling. Bob would answer, "Oh, I am doing fine." The nurse and I looked at each other and laughed because we had watched him struggle throughout the day. After that, Dr. Lynch would first ask us how he was doing.

But Bob's positive attitude would be tested further. About the time he was released from the hospital, he was diagnosed with congestive heart failure. He could only walk a few steps before he would have to sit down to rest. Going up and down the stairs in our condo got so difficult for him that he had to sleep on the sofa downstairs. He went to cardiac rehab three times a week for three months. Through a lot of hard work, Bob's heart function was back to normal.

When Bob went in to see his primary care doctor, he looked at Bob's chart for the six months he was in the hospital. He said that he had an impressive list of the best doctors in their specialty and in about every medical field. That basically summed up what he had been through. But the important thing is that Bob made it through each crisis and was released from most of the specialists, except for his heart doctor and oncologist.

The average hospital stay for a bone marrow transplant was much shorter than Bob's. Before the transplant, we were shown a list of possible side effects that he might or might not have. Unfortunately, Bob experienced a lot of them, but God gave us the strength to endure. In the years since, there have been a lot of changes and improvements in treatments.

We were so thankful for Bob's HMO insurance policy that paid for his spleen surgery, chemo, radiation, long hospital stay, medications, cardiac rehab, and all of his other many medical expenses. During the first few months after his transplant, I received a letter with a list of hospital expenses for a total of $116,000 for that month. After the initial shock, I quickly called the hospital, and they said that insurance was being billed, so we would not have to pay for it. I never received any more notices after that, so I can only imagine what the total charges might have been for the six-month hospital stay.

In November, Bob's dad, Jim, drove from Florida to take Dot back home. Finally, we were ready for some sense of normalcy in our lives and marriage.

11

A Time of Healing

IT WASN'T LONG before Bob was able to get back to doing the things that he enjoyed. He was glad to be working again at his agency, Helping Hands of Tulsa. It was through the help of all the staff and the board of directors that everything kept running smoothly while he was gone for that length of time. The program director would come up to the hospital to go over the daily operations with Bob. Then I would deliver the paperwork to the secretary at the office for him.

Three years later, due to the economy, Bob's agency and another like agency merged to form the new nonprofit named Youth at Heart. At that time, he stepped down as executive director and took a position as recreation director. Jocelyn, the executive director of the other organization, was able to continue on in that same capacity. Bob realized it was the best move for the new nonprofit. The merger went smoothly, and Youth at Heart continued to impact the lives of the city's youth.

Bob with Youth at Heart sports activity

Bob with Youth at Heart tennis activity

Bob was also able to get back to playing his beloved game of tennis with his brother again. I still remember watching them play for the first time after Bob's illness. They were both smiling from ear to ear. This was a true statement to all three of us that Bob was back to himself again.

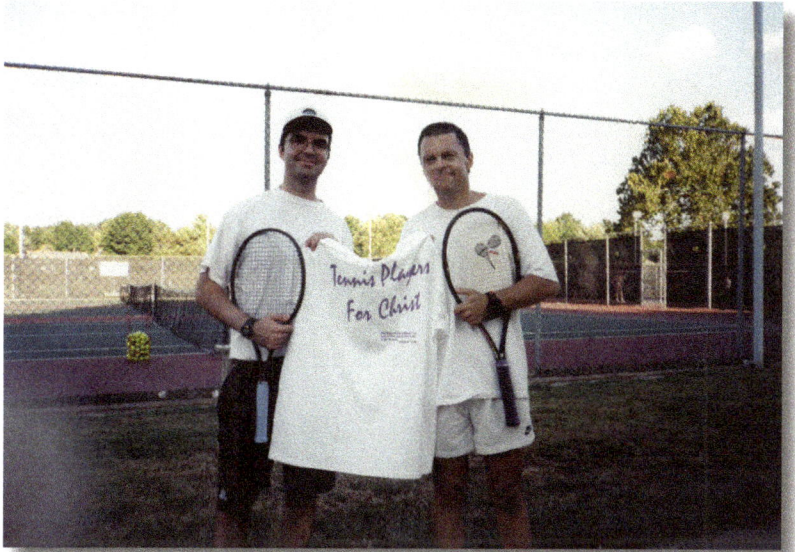

Brothers Ron and Bob back playing tennis

The next year, Ron met and married Leah, the music teacher at his school. Bob's family arrived for the special occasion. It was good to see everyone again as we celebrated Ron's special day and Bob's renewed health. A couple of years later, Ron and Leah moved to Dallas where they had new teaching positions.

When the next school year arrived, Bob decided to go back into refereeing high school basketball in the evenings. Again we saw how far God had brought him that last year.

But Bob didn't forget how grateful he was to get through this difficult time, and he wanted to give back. When he went for his checkups with his oncologist, whose office was next to the hospital,

Bob would visit the bone marrow unit to encourage the patients. I think it blessed Bob as much as it did them.

When you get to the top of your mountain and are enjoying the view, look down, and you may see others who are climbing the same mountain. If you take time out of sightseeing, from your vantage point, you can help guide and encourage them to finish their climb, always remembering to keep looking upward. It is always helpful to hear from someone who has gone before you because you know they truly understand what you are going through and can give you important insights. When you bless others, you always receive a great blessing in return.

With each visit to Dr. Lynch, Bob would get another report of being in remission. Each spring the doctor has a Celebration of Life get-together for all his bone marrow transplant patients. After dinner, the doctor and nurses call the cancer survivors by name and announce how many years they have been cancer-free and have them come forward to receive a Celebration of Life gift. Their donors are also honored for their willingness to sacrifice. We enjoy going to this event each year. We get to talk to others who have been through similar trials.

We spent our fourth wedding anniversary in Binghamton, New York, where Bob grew up and where his sister, Barbara, still lives. All of his family including aunts, uncles, and cousins were there to celebrate Bob's parents' fiftieth wedding anniversary. I enjoyed seeing where he was raised and meeting all his relatives.

Bob and his siblings Barbara, Kathleen, and Ron, with
their parents Dot and Jim at their fiftieth anniversary

Then Bob took me on a scenic drive up the east side of the
state through the Adirondack Mountains and state park. We toured
the Ausable Chasm as we walked on trails down the side of the cliff
overlooking the roaring Ausable River.

Then I thoroughly enjoyed a ferry boat ride across Lake
Champlain to Burlington, Vermont, where Bob's family moved when
he was in the tenth grade. We stayed at a nice hotel in a corner room
that had a gorgeous 190-degree view of the tranquil lake nestled in
the beautiful mountains.

Bob took me to see his family home. Then he showed me where
he would walk to the back of his neighborhood and onto a beach
that overlooked Lake Champlain. He would take his dog, Ginger,
and throw a ball into the lake for her to eagerly retrieve from the
water.

He gave me a tour of all the sights in that area, including his
high school, the University of Vermont where he received a business
degree, Trinity College where he taught the women's tennis team

for five years, and the tennis club where he worked as a pro tennis instructor.

Bob's dad requested that we go to the marina where his old sailboat, the *Yellow Jacket*, was docked. Bob's dad, Jim, raced his beloved boat on Lake Champlain where he won the Mayor's Cup between New York State and Vermont. Since I have always been fascinated by sailboats, I was excited to fulfill Jim's request.

The owner of the marina said they were honored for the time that they were able to store Jim's boat, but the new owners had moved it to a marina farther south. We went on a scenic drive alongside the lake in search of Jim's treasured *Yellow Jacket*, which was anchored out in the harbor. I was disappointed that I had to view it from a distance, but I was glad that we had found it still in fine shape so I could give the good report back to Jim.

The next day, we drove to Stowe where we toured Ben and Jerry's Ice Cream Factory, a store where they made maple syrup, Vermont's Teddy Bear Factory, the Von Trapp Family Lodge, and drove through a covered bridge. Bob ended our sightseeing with a ski lift ride to the top of Mount Mansfield to take in the beautiful scenery. I was grateful to be able to see where Bob lived as he shared his old memories with me, and we made new ones together.

A year later, we decided that after living in the condo for five years, it was time to buy a house. It was important to stay close to my parents. I decided to drive through the addition next to our condo. I found a one-story house for sale that was on the end of a cul-de-sac. I couldn't wait to call our realtor for a tour of the house.

I knew when I first set foot inside that it was to be our next home. It had a big patio in the back overlooking a green belt, and to the north was a pond that was full of ducks and geese. When the geese flew overhead, I felt like I was on vacation. There was also a view of the pond from the kitchen window. I always dreamed of living by a lake, so this was close to fulfilling that dream. The house needed some updating that we agreed could be done over time. We closed on the house and moved in on June 1. That gave me the summer to get settled into our home.

At the end of the summer, we were informed that enrollment was very low at the Christian school where I taught third grade. The pastor decided that it was too late to close the school, so they would stay open for one more year before closing. That year I taught a combined third and fourth grade class. We made the best of the last year and tried to make it memorable for the students.

During Christmas vacation, my mother slipped on the icy sidewalk as she was going to her mailbox. I took her to the doctor, and unfortunately, she broke her shoulder and needed surgery to put in a pin.

She said she knew that it was time to put Dad in a nursing home, but it was hard for her to make that decision until this happened, and she had no choice. In addition to his Alzheimer's and colostomy bag, Dad had become blind and was very hard of hearing, which had made it even more challenging for Mom to care for him. She and I both wondered how she was able to take care of Dad for as long as she did. But Mom was a hard worker, and I had always admired her for all that she was able to accomplish.

Most nursing homes have a long waiting list, but the one that had been recommended to us happened to have an opening. We were able to get Dad admitted and settled into his room in time to take Mom to the hospital for surgery. Her operation went well, and she recovered quickly with the help of physical therapy. Dad adjusted well to his new home, and we were very pleased with the nice facility and the helpful staff.

Then the final year of my school came to an end. We celebrated the last day with a program and awards assembly that honored the students and teachers, a special luncheon with parents, and a balloon release.

It took me several days to get my teacher supplies packed up and loaded in my car and the schoolbooks and equipment ready for the church's school audition. I took one last look around the bare classroom that had been filled for years with colorful bulletin boards and cheerful third graders. A flood of fond memories filled my mind as I closed the door and walked down the hall for the last time after twenty-five years. I thought that it would be overwhelmingly sad, but instead, I left in peace. I knew it was time to leave, and there would be another open door ahead for me.

Bob and I never made it to Corpus Christi after his transplant, but he decided to take me on a trip to Hawaii that summer. It gave me something to look forward to during the school closing. We took a cruise of the four major Hawaiian islands. It was a relaxing and fun trip. We continued to enjoy our time together making more great memories.

I substituted for a year, which gave me some time to rest up. Then I was hired as a third grade teacher at the Christian school at our church. Transitioning to a new school can be a big adjustment, but I thoroughly enjoyed it there.

A year later, I felt that it was time to get a dog. I saw the breed Cavalier King Charles spaniel on TV, and after reading about it, I knew it was the breed for us. I even had a name ready for the new pet. I always liked the name Gracie, and since I had never been able to use it for a child, I decided that it would be the name of our soon-to-be new family member.

We answered an ad in the paper and drove to see the dog. At the entry of the apartment, the owner had us walk up a flight of stairs to the living room. As we looked up to the top of the stairs, we were met by this adorable six-month-old puppy whose big brown eyes eagerly greeted us. She had a striking coat of black and white with a little brown, which is referred to as tricolored. She bounced up and down and flipped around and around, anxiously awaiting our arrival at the top of the stairs. We knew immediately that we had to have her.

After we got everything ready for Gracie, we came back to get her and take her home with us. When we opened the car door, she willingly entered her new crate with a soft bed and settled in for the ride to her new home. When we saw how well she rode in a car, we knew that she would be able to handle our trips to Dallas to visit Ron's family.

I told my third grade class about our new puppy. One of my students, Jared, asked if Gracie had obedience training. Then he told me that his mom taught classes at their home. I was so surprised that I had him repeat what he had just said.

We were able to get Gracie in the next class at Top Dog Training, which was starting soon. Bob and I both enjoyed working with Gracie at the classes. When she had completed all of the training, they had a graduation for the dogs. We brought my mom to see all that Gracie had learned and to watch her receive her certificate.

There was a second obedience class that summer that we wanted Gracie to attend, but we were unaware of all the upcoming events in store for us that summer.

12

Another Mountain

EIGHT YEARS AFTER the transplant and the last week before school let out for the summer, I got a call that Bob was taken to the emergency room at Saint Francis Hospital because he was not feeling well. The next day at my school's awards assembly, I was very concerned for Bob and wondered what lay ahead for us.

That summer, Bob was in the hospital five times. Once he had a serious infection, and another time he had pneumonia. The last time he was hospitalized was in August, and I was attending a local teacher conference. I got a call that a doctor at the hospital wanted to talk to me. I left the meeting and rushed to the hospital wondering what news I would receive this time.

Bob's heart doctor, Dr. Ross, informed me that Bob had relapsed into congestive heart failure. Since it was not as severe this time as before, Bob was just treated with medicine. He was also diagnosed with mild kidney failure. He would have to go to a kidney doctor for routine visits to monitor his kidney function.

We received this information the week before school started. While we were preparing for the new school year, I was informed that I would be moved up to fourth grade. So I packed up my supplies and moved them to my new classroom to begin setting up for the new grade. I had to quickly come up with new bulletin board ideas. I gathered up the teacher's guides for each subject I would be teaching and took them home to study and do lesson plans.

After twenty-two years of teaching third grade, it was a nice change for me. But changing to a different grade level is a lot of work, and I didn't know that there would be more challenges during that school year.

Bob had to adjust to his new health issues. He soon realized that he could no longer continue to play tennis or referee basketball. It was a hard but necessary decision for him to make. A year or two later, he was diagnosed with diabetes, which required a big change in diet. We attended informative classes that helped us to understand how to deal with his new illness.

In January, my loving father died from Alzheimer's. He had been in the nursing home for about four years. He did not know who we were anymore. It was hard to see him slipping away from us. It was as though we had been saying good-bye for years, and finally at least we could have closure. Then I could remember him for the smart and caring father that he was before this disease had stolen him from us.

The week after the funeral, Bob had to have cataract surgery on both of his eyes. Not only could Bob see better, but since the eye doctor also put artificial lens in his eyes, Bob did not have to wear eyeglasses anymore.

Bob started showing symptoms of Parkinson's disease, but we had to wait for over a month for an appointment to see the specialist. The doctor was ready to put him on Parkinson's medication because there was not a test for it. Then I asked if it could be a side effect from one of his new medications. The doctor left the room to look it up. Sure enough, when he came back, he agreed that it could be due to one of Bob's prescriptions. When the medicine was changed, we were relieved that the symptoms had subsided.

That summer, due to low enrollment, I lost my teaching position in the private Christian school where I had taught for three years. The next year, the school kept me busy substituting, but by that summer, unfortunately, the school had to close.

After going through two school closings, I knew I did not have the strength to start all over again. So I decided I was ready to retire after thirty-seven years of teaching, even though I would not receive state teachers' retirement from a private school. It would be two years before I could receive early retirement at sixty-two, but I knew it was time.

In May, I gave my beloved mom a surprise ninetieth birthday party at the park. It was a special day. On the drive home, Mom kept saying what a nice surprise it was and that she just couldn't believe we had done that for her.

By the end of the summer, Mom told me that she didn't know how much longer she could live alone and take care of everything herself. So I started going through her things to get ready for an estate sale. Bob and I got our guest room ready for her, and that fall, we moved her in to live with us. I was glad that I was not working and could be there to care for her.

Gracie was also happy to have this special family member staying with us. She was careful to not get in the way of Mom's walker. When I helped her get in bed, Gracie would jump up beside Mom to help me say good night to her.

Mom lived with us for four months before she passed away two months short of her ninety-first birthday. We enjoyed having her in our home. She is so greatly missed.

Exactly a year later, I finally found an organization where I could get our dog, Gracie, certified as a therapy dog so I could take her to a school for the dog reading program. The elementary students read to the dogs to help improve their confidence and enjoyment in reading.

Gracie and I had to be observed three times as a team to pass certification requirements. The first place to be observed was Clarehouse, a hospice residence and end-of-life care center. I was very nervous because I wasn't sure how Gracie would do and how the visit might affect me. When we walked into the first room, I knew that this was what we were called to do. Our first patient was there for two months. She looked forward to Thursdays when our dogs came for a visit. She helped to show me that what we were doing did make a difference. We not only visited with patients, but we were also there for their families. I understood what they were going through.

Since Gracie received her certification, we have continued to visit there each week. Visiting the sick is not what I would have chosen, and it is not my gift. But it is Gracie's gift. She does the visiting, and I just assist her as I lift her onto the bed. Her big brown eyes and eagerness to make a new friend lifts their spirits. There is nothing like a pet to cheer you up and brighten your day.

When I saw how much we were blessing others during a difficult time, it blessed me in return and helped me through my second phase of healing in the grieving process of losing my mom.

The next fall I found a school, Immanuel Lutheran Christian Academy, that was interested in having Gracie and me volunteer once a week for the dog reading program with Mrs. Long's and Mrs. Schultz's kindergarten classes. Since I was retired from teaching, this gave me the opportunity to be back in the classroom doing what I have always loved, which is working with children. Except this time it was with Gracie by my side to get their attention with a wag of her tail.

Through all our trials and challenges, Bob and I were reminded again that God was our comfort and strength.

13

The Party

AFTER REFLECTING BACK on the last sixteen years of marriage, I was so thankful to be planning Bob's sixtieth birthday party. I met Bob's mom at the airport, and we eagerly set out to finish last-minute details for the party the next day, Saturday, March 21, 2015.

When we got home, I had Dot stay in the kitchen. I told Bob to come and see the birthday surprise that I had for him in the other room. Bob was very surprised and thrilled to see that his mom had come for his birthday, but he still had no idea of what else I had planned.

On the big day, his coworker, Rodney, called Bob and asked him to stop by the office to sign some papers. Bob did not want to leave his mom, so Dot and I offered to ride with him to work. Bob did not know that I had my friend Patty set up the meeting room for the party, where everyone was waiting for us.

Bob was so pleasantly surprised and delighted to see friends, family, and coworkers who came to celebrate with him. His brother Ron came from Dallas with his daughter, Kimmie, who even surprised her grandma. Ron also brought Bob's close friend, Bill, who helped Bob start Helping Hands of Tulsa.

After we had birthday cake and fruit, we watched a touching slide presentation of Bob's life that Zach, the son of my friend Amy, had put together for the occasion.

I was so relieved that the party was such a success and that I had managed somehow to keep it all a secret. Bob gratefully appreciated that I did all this for him. And I was thankful to everyone for helping to make this day special for Bob.

Again, we did not know what would be ahead for us in the next several months.

14

Our Climb Continues

FIVE MONTHS LATER, in August, Bob called to let me know that he was coming home from work because of chest pains. His doctor told him to go to the emergency room. Bob was admitted to Saint Francis Hospital and was scheduled for a heart cath procedure the next morning.

I got to his room early, but I was told that Bob had just been taken down to the first floor to get ready for the procedure. The nurse said if I hurried that I might catch up with them on the way down. But I was not fast enough and was disappointed that I did not get to see Bob.

While I was sitting in the waiting room, I started feeling weak and light-headed. I told the receptionist, and immediately, I was swarmed with hospital staff all around me. They said I needed to be admitted to the emergency room because my blood pressure was extremely low, and I was dehydrated. The ER doctor was surprised to see me again because this time I was the patient. I called my good friend Valerie, and she dropped everything and immediately drove up to be there with me in my room.

While I was receiving IV fluids, Bob's doctor came to the emergency room to give me the results of the heart cath procedure. To my surprise, it revealed that Bob needed a quadruple bypass heart surgery. I was glad that Valerie was there because it was reassuring to have a friend there to lean on during a time when I did not feel strong enough to handle it on my own.

Later that day, I was released from the emergency room, but Bob had to wait in the hospital for a week before they could perform his surgery because he had been on a blood thinner.

On the day of the operation, my longtime friend Clois and her husband, Wayne, met me at the hospital to keep me company. I was glad to have someone to talk with during the long wait. The open-heart surgery was a success, and five days later, Bob was dismissed from the hospital.

Two days after he came home, I walked into the room to help Bob get ready for bed. He had just lain down and gotten comfortable. I was ready to turn around and leave the room when I noticed his arm go limp and that he had stopped breathing. I realized that Bob had had a cardiac arrest. I frantically ran to get the phone from the living room even though I did not want to leave him. Then I called 911 as I began mouth-to-mouth breathing. Gracie nervously watched me as she sat next to Bob.

The emergency team arrived quickly and began working on Bob. As I tried to put Gracie in her crate, she slipped away from me and made a mad dash to the other room to get to her beloved master. Just as she squeezed between two paramedics, I was able to grab her and take her back to her crate. The team was able to successfully resuscitate Bob, but he was still unconscious when they transported him back to the hospital. It was about 11:30 p.m., and I was too shook up to drive to the hospital, so two of my neighbors, Kim and Cheryl, offered to take me.

Then I decided it would be best to wait until morning to go to the hospital. I continued to get weaker and could hardly talk. The 911 paramedics were called out again, but this time it was for me. They checked me out and said that I probably had a panic attack. They suggested that it would be best for me to not be alone that night.

When the paramedics left and Gracie was let out of her crate again, she was so glad to see that I was still there. Kim and Cheryl kept me company until my retired friends, Clois and Wayne, drove in from thirty minutes out of town to stay with me that night. They were such an encouragement to me. Around 2:00 a.m., Bob's heart doctor, Dr. Ross, called to tell me that he had put in a temporary pacemaker, but he would not know for a while if there had been any brain damage.

That morning, Clois and Wayne had to leave for a doctor's appointment. I had only about one hour of sleep, so I was glad that my close friend Valerie, who lives fifty minutes from me, came to drive me to the hospital to visit Bob. Since he was still unconscious, it was a great comfort to have her there.

Finally, to my great relief, I was informed that Bob did not suffer any brain damage. Later, they removed the temporary pacemaker and were going to run tests on Monday morning to see if he needed a permanent one. During the night before, he had another cardiac arrest, and a nurse promptly did CPR and resuscitated him. That morning, Bob received a permanent pacemaker.

On the day that Bob was again released from the hospital, his brother Ron came from Dallas for the weekend and was a great help to us. He willingly cleaned Bob's fish tank and gladly made a run in the mornings to get breakfast burritos for his big brother. It was a comfort and relief to me to have Ron there because of what had happened the last time Bob came home.

A few weeks later, Bob returned to work, and after a week, he began cardiac rehab. Three weeks later he started having chest pains again, so I took him back to the emergency room. Tests showed that scar issue had developed where an artery had been grafted to bypass one of the clotted arteries. So they put in a stent to keep the scarred graft open.

Again Bob returned home and continued cardiac rehab. During the first month of rehab, we attended education classes, which were very informative. After the class Bob would work out on the equipment for an hour as his heart was being monitored. The rehab nurses were so helpful and encouraging. We also enjoyed getting acquainted with the other patients and their families as we would share each other's stories.

Nine days after his last visit to the hospital, he had more chest pains, so we returned to the emergency room. This time they decided to treat it with medication, and Bob was released from the hospital after three days.

There are no words to completely express our appreciation to the paramedic team and nurse who saved Bob's life by resuscitation and for all of the wonderful care he received from the hospital, doctors, nurses, and staff during all of his stays at Saint Francis Hospital. Bob survived three heart attacks and was brought back to life twice from cardiac arrests. Sometimes even during the most trying of circumstances, God still has a plan, a purpose, and a work for you to do.

Since Bob's Uncle John from North Carolina had gone through the same bypass surgery, he would call to check on how Bob was doing. His calls were a comfort to Bob because he knew that his uncle understood completely what he was going through. Bob also received calls from Uncle John's two sons, John and Kevin, who were an encouragement to him.

We were so thankful for our family, friends, and neighbors who were there to give Bob and me the help and strength we needed to get through another difficult period. This reminded me of the story in the Bible when Moses lifted his hands and rod during the battle with Amalek so Israel would prevail. When his arms got tired, Aaron and Hur stood on either side of him and held them up for him.

This story came alive for me during this most challenging time. I felt like Moses when I was too weary to keep going; God provided my Aaron and Hur to be there beside me to help keep me lifted up during an incredibly tough several months.

15

Valley of Rest

BOB WAS RELEASED from his last hospital visit a week before Thanksgiving. We usually drive to Ron and Leah's near Dallas for Thanksgiving, but Bob knew he was not ready for a four-and-a-half-hour ride. So we decided to spend it with my family because they live closer. But Bob realized that he was not strong enough to even make a two-and-a-half-hour trip. We canceled our plans and spent Thanksgiving week by ourselves, resting up from the last three months.

During December, Bob got stronger every day. On Christmas Day we were able to make the drive to spend the holiday with my family. Due to the forecast of freezing rain and sleet, we had to cut the trip short and travel back home the next morning. I drove through thunderstorms and heavy fog, but we were glad to arrive home before the temperatures dropped and covered the trees and roads with ice.

On December 28, Ron, Leah, and Kimmie came to spend three days with us. It was so good to see them. We were so thankful to be able to spend the Christmas holiday with our families.

Bob and I celebrated Valentine's Day at the same Italian restaurant where he proposed to me seventeen years before. At that time, the doctor had said that Bob might have only three or four years to live, and most of those would be rough years.

At Bob's annual checkup with Dr. Lynch, his blood test revealed that he was sixteen years cancer-free. We are thankful for every good report and believe that they will continue in the future.

In March we drove to Dallas to see Bob's brother and his family. Since Bob is a big hockey fan, Ron took him to watch the Dallas Stars play the LA Kings because they are two of Bob's favorite teams. This was a perfect gift for Bob's sixty-first birthday.

While we were there, Ron drove us to see the lot where his family's new house was being built in a Dallas suburb to be closer to Leah's and Kimmie's schools. Since it was a four-bedroom house, they invited Dot to move in with them. Because Jim had gone into a nursing home in the last year due to progressing Alzheimer's, we also toured a memory care facility for him.

Bob had to attend a United States Tennis Association Workshop the first weekend of April in Los Angeles, California. He had me fly out with him. It was mainly a time of rest for me, but Bob had a busy schedule. He enjoyed the workshop, and we had a good flight there and back. He had to show his pacemaker ID to go through security at the airport, but everything went smoothly.

As we boarded the plane, I fought Bob for the window seat so I could be entertained by the view. I always marvel at the different perspective we have of life from above. Everything seems so much smaller. The large mountain ranges appear to be no more than mounds of dirt and rocks. If only we could see our problems from this prospective, we might approach them differently.

As we arrived home, it was encouraging to see how well Bob had handled the trip, and it showed that he was continuing to get stronger.

We attended the annual Celebration of Life event again in May, which was at the zoo. It was good to visit with Dr. Lynch and the staff and catch them up on the latest of how Bob was doing. We also met patients and their families and shared our experiences with each other and how thankful we were for the great care that we received. This annual event makes us feel like we are all a part of a special family.

We were very thankful for Bob's continuing recovery, for times of rest, and for God's healing power, both physically and mentally.

16

Looking Forward

IN JULY, RON and Leah's house was completed, and they were able to move into their beautiful new home. Dot was able to quickly sell her house in Florida, and in August, she and Jim flew to Dallas. He was transferred to the memory care center there, and she moved in with Ron and his family. Now, when Bob and I go to Ron and Leah's for Thanksgiving, we will also get to visit with Bob's parents. It is nice to have Dot and Jim closer to us.

We celebrated our seventeen years of marriage on June 19. Since Bob was busy with work during the summer, we waited until the last week of August to go on an anniversary getaway at Lake Tenkiller for a few days with our dog, Gracie. It also happened to be the one-year anniversary since Bob's open-heart surgery. Again we were so thankful after all we had been through that we were able to celebrate another year together.

Because school had started and it was during the middle of the week, it was very quiet and tranquil there. We went on walks with Gracie to take in the serene setting of a pond with four white ducks, the calm lake below us, and the peaceful hills around us.

For dinner I drove us down a curvy and hilly road to a local café. We were startled as a graceful deer leaped across the road, over the fence, and into the woods. Bob told me to slow down because there may be another deer. As he had forecasted, the female swiftly followed the lead of the male. Again, Bob told me to wait. As predicted, we saw a small fawn dart quickly in front of us. As I drove on, I asked Bob to look back to see if the deer was watching us pass by. As he turned around, Bob reported that he saw the fawn staring safely from the other side of the fence before it took off into the trees.

Amazed at what we had just witnessed, we continued on to the café. After dinner we returned to our comfortable cabin and cherished the time to be able to just rest and focus on each other with Gracie beside us.

Even with all that had happened since last August, Gracie and I continued volunteering once a week, when possible, with hospice and the school reading program, where we are now working with second graders. These visits with Clarehouse and Immanuel Lutheran Christian Academy helped keep my mind from dwelling on all that was going on by encouraging others. Again, Gracie assisted me in dealing with a difficult time in my life.

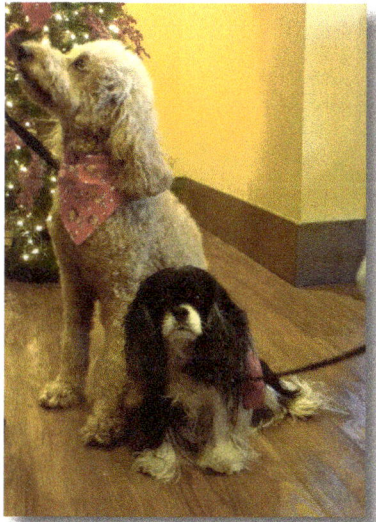

Therapy dogs Gracie and Lucy ready for Clarehouse visit

Second grader Nolen reads to Gracie.

I can't believe that Gracie is now nine years old, even though she still acts like a puppy. For three years she has had a heart murmur and enlarged heart. The vet specialist recently informed me that she is very close to having congestive heart failure.

She is still able to take daily walks with me around our neighborhood. She wants to meet everyone, and she would even like to be friends with all of the cats if they would let her. She knows where the neighbor dogs and children live, and when we walk by their house, she thinks we should go to their door to say hello. Gracie enjoys the days when my neighbors Emma, her brother Ethan, and their cousin Missy stop by to see Gracie and take her for walks.

Illustrated by Emma, age 9

Illustrated by Missy, age 11

Even though she has not slowed down yet, I realize that it won't be long before I will be paying Gracie back for all she has done for me by helping her through a rough period.

Bob's job at Youth at Heart is going well. He thoroughly enjoys working with Jocelyn, president and CEO; Rodney, director of Program Management; Kelvin, director of Enrichment Programs; Marquetta, director of Development; and Roy, volunteer coordinator. As director of Sports Programming, Bob does tennis clinics with the youth in the spring, summer, and fall and also helps in the after school program.

Bob continues to gain strength. We have been told by his Uncle John and others who have been through bypass surgery that it can take up to a year to get back to normal. I feel that it was Bob's positive attitude and athletic mind-set that helped him beat the norm and will continue to help him fight through whatever the future brings.

Bob and I are so grateful for the years that we have had together and are cherishing each moment we have now and will have in the future. We know you cannot take anything for granted.

We do not know what lies ahead for us, but we do know that as we glance back to realize how far God has brought us, we can look forward with certainty that He has not brought us this far to leave us, but is here to guide us on our continuing journey. We plan to just enjoy the view along the way, always be thankful to God, and never forget to appreciate each other.

> "Blessed is the man who perseveres under trial" (James 1:12, NIV).

> "We count them happy which endure" (James 5:11, KJV).

Epilogue

AROUND TWENTY YEARS ago I wrote a poem that God put on my heart to encourage a friend who was waiting for a soul mate. I took one line from what another friend once said, "As we are serving God, one day we will look beside us and see someone else serving God and going in the same direction as we are."

It is important to be content with where we are at the present to be able to see God's best for us in the future.

Soon after I wrote the poem, it came true for me. Two years after I married Bob, I was invited to a wedding shower for my friend. At about that time, I happened to come upon my first draft of the poem. I bought a double picture frame. On one side I placed the poem and I left the other side ready for their wedding picture.

Then I realized that God not only gave me the poem for them, but it was also for me. So I made another copy and placed it in a frame that I received for my wedding. It is still hanging in our home as a reminder of God's perfect plan and timing for our lives.

May this poem be an encouragement to others?

Tomorrow's Dreams

It is all right to dream
God sees our biggest dreams
God knows all of the desires of our heart,
As He holds our tomorrows in His hands

It is all right to dream for tomorrow
As we keep our eyes on Him today
As we are serving Him in faith,
God will hand us our tomorrow's dreams today

We will know it is from Him,
Because it will be more
Than we could ever dream!

Barbara J. Corcoran

About the Author

BARBARA J. CORCORAN was born and raised in central Oklahoma. She received a bachelor of science degree in elementary education from East Central State University at Ada, Oklahoma, in 1972.

A first grade teaching position brought her to the Tulsa area in 1974. After six years in the public school system, she felt called to teach in the private Christian schools. In 2011, after teaching grades first through fourth for thirty-seven years, she retired from the occupation that she dearly loved.

She took two summer mission trips to China and the Philippines in 1994 and 1996. In the summer of 1995, she taught oral English at a police academy in China. These three trips had a great impact on her life and prepared her for the challenges that she would be faced with in the future.

In 1999, she married Bob Corcoran. For years friends encouraged her to write a book about their inspiring story.

Finally, after seventeen years of marriage, she found the words to begin documenting their life together. Then she moved forward to publish her first book with the hope that it may help to encourage others going through similar trials.

MICHAEL PRIDE
918 740 - 3121

99

CPSIA information can be obtained
at www.ICGtesting.com
Printed in the USA
LVHW07s1427240418
574673LV00027B/321/P

9 781635 759723